Your Lie in April

*I met the girl
under full-bloomed cherry blossoms,
and my fate has begun to change.*

3

Naoshi Arakawa

✿ STORY & CHARACTERS ✿

✿ Kōsei Arima

An ex-piano prodigy who lost his ability to play when his mother died. He can't hear the sound of the piano when he concentrates on his performance.

YOU ARE FREEDOM ITSELF.

SOME-THING DRIVES US...

...TO PERFORM.

✿ Kaori Miyazono

A violinist who is overwhelmingly unique. In the second round of her violin competition, she captivated the audience with a musicians' duel against Kōsei.

✿ Tsubaki Sawabe

The school softball team's power hitter. A longtime friend and next-door neighbor of Kōsei. Saitō-sempai, the boy she admired from the baseball team, has asked her to go out with him.

WHAT ARE YOU DOING NOW, SEMPAI?

✿ Ryōta Watari

Captain of the soccer team and longtime friend of Kōsei and Tsubaki. Girls love him, and he loves girls. People call him superficial, but sometimes he says things that are pretty deep.

I'LL NEVER FORGET IT.

I HAVE THAT IMAGE OF YOU TWO BURNED INTO MY MEMORY.

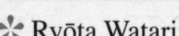

When his mother died in the autumn of his 12th year, piano prodigy Kōsei Arima lost his ability to play.

Without a purpose, his days lost all color and continued on in a drab monotone. But in the spring when he was 14, he met a girl who began to change his dreary world: the cheerfully violent, exceedingly ill-tempered, and exceptionally talented violinist Kaori Miyazono. As he watches her joyous performance, Kōsei finds himself drawn to her.

At Kaori's request, Kōsei agreed to accompany her in the second round of the Tōwa Music Competition. He pushed through his inability to hear the music and gave a powerful performance. The audience showered them with applause.

Immediately afterward, Kaori fainted, worrying Kōsei and his friends. But Kaori told them that she was only put in the hospital for tests, and, as his gift to celebrate her release, she ordered Kōsei to enter a piano competition!

contents

Chapter 9: The Cassette Recording and the Moon

ギ ギ
ギ …
HMM

STOMP

I COULD GET YOU SOME WARM MILK, TOO.

IS COFFEE OKAY?

HERE YOU ARE.

RRR AAA GAH

FWOOSH

CRASH

AIEEE!

RUSTLE

WH—WH—WHAT ARE YOU—?!

I'M SORRY.

FORGET IT.

SHE WANTS ME TO ENTER A COMPETITION LIKE THIS?!

GLOOM ず〜ん

IS THAT MY WALLET?!

?!

I ALREADY SENT IN YOUR APPLICATION.

SO WHAT KIND OF A TOURNAMENT ARE WE TALKING ABOUT?

YOU PAID THE ENTRY FEE?!

THE MAIHŌ MUSIC COMPETITION!

AND! LOTS OF FAMOUS MUSICIANS STARTED OUT BY WINNING THERE!

IT'S A NATIONAL COMPETITION THAT MAIHŌ SHIMBUNSHA SPONSORS EVERY YEAR!

WATARI! TSUBAKI!

KASHIWAGISAN?

WHOA.

WOW.

IT STARTS WITH THE DISTRICT PRELIMINARIES, THEN THE DISTRICT COMPETITION, AND THEN YOU GO ON TO NATIONALS.

IF YOU WIN...

...THEN IT'S YOUR FIRST STEP TO INTERNATIONAL STARDOM.

INTERNATIONAL.

PROFESSIONAL.

...JUST 14-YEAR-OLD KIDS.

BUT WE'RE ALL...

...SOUND LIKE THEY'RE FROM A FAR OFF WORLD.

ALL THESE THINGS KAO-CHAN IS TALKING ABOUT...

!

YOUR TEACHER...

SHUDDER

I NEED TO FIND MYSELF A TEACHER.

YOU'LL BE FINE. YOU HAVE ALL THE TECHNIQUES DOWN.

GLOOM

INCIDENTALLY, THIS YOUNG MAN...

...HAS WON FIRST PLACE IN THE COMPETITION'S ELEMENTARY SCHOOL DIVISION.

WHAT?!

"BEFORE YOUR FINGERS TOUCH THE KEYS...

...YOU MUST BEGIN THE PIECE *MENTALLY*."

ANTON RUBIN-STEIN*.

*ANTON RUBINSTEIN (1829-1894): A RUSSIAN COMPOSER, PIANIST, AND CONDUCTOR.

HEART. 心 は MUSIC

IS ♪

FOR SOME-ONE ELSE?

FOR YOUR-SELF?

WHAT ARE YOU PLAYING THE PIANO FOR?

HOW DO YOU WANT TO PLAY BACH?

HOW...

...DO YOU WANT TO PLAY THIS PIECE?

ZOOM

I'LL PLAY MY HARD-EST!

EEEEEE!

YOU SMELL SO SWEATY!

I'M GONNA GO WATCH WATARI-KUN PRACTICE.

OUR BREAK'S GONNA BE OVER!

DROP DEAD.

YOU TWO KEEP AT IT!

ALOOONE

WELL.

...YOU AND ME AGAIN.

IT'S JUST...

WHAT ARE YOU VISUALIZING?

VISUALIZE.

IMAGINE.

A HORSE-DRAWN CARRIAGE TRAVELING THE STONY PATHS OF EUROPE—

TOO CLICHÉ!

WHERE'S YOUR IMAGINATION?!

ISMAK

?!

Music Room

ZOMBIE?!

SHAMBLE

SHAMBLE

VISU-ALIZE.

KŌSEI?!

TSU-BAKI

SMACK!

チ

TOO ORDINARY! NO ROMANCE!

A FRIED EGG FOR BREAKF—

SHUFFLE

の

はっ ちっ ...

I'M THIRSTY ...

HUH?

NO WAY!

AM 02:41

...STILL PLAYING?

IS KŌSEI...

HOW'S THE DISTRICT TOURNAMENT LOOKING?

WE'RE TOTALLY READY! AS LONG AS NOBODY GETS INJURED.

THERE WAS SMOKE COMING FROM ARIMA-KUN'S HEAD THE OTHER DAY.

BUT I THINK HE'S STARTING TO SEE IT.

WHAT ABOUT YOU?

HE'S BEEN PLAYING NON-STOP FOR DAYS.

AND HE WAS SHAMBLING DOWN THE HALLS.

HE EVEN FORGETS TO EAT.

...

I WONDER IF HE'S WORKING HIMSELF TOO HARD.

I WANT HIM TO PLAY THE PIANO.

RIGHT NOW, ARIMA-KUN...

...IS TRYING TO TURN THAT PAIN INTO MUSIC.

...I DON'T WANT IT TO BE PAINFUL FOR HIM.

BUT...

THAT'S...

THAT'S HOW...

...WE PUT OURSELVES INTO THE SOUND.

WE TAKE THE PAIN, THE SUFFERING—

WE PUT ALL OUR STRUGGLES OUT THERE FOR EVERYONE TO SEE.

...HOW OUR MUSIC COMES ALIVE.

AND PUT THEM ON THE STRINGS.

...IS DOING RIGHT NOW.

I BET THAT'S WHAT ARIMA-KUN...

"WE."

...DEFENDING HIM LIKE THAT?

...WHY ARE YOU ALWAYS...

KAO-CHAN...

I DON'T KNOW. I GUESS ...

HMMM.

WHISPER

KŌSEI...

...IS *NOT* HOPE-LESS.

...HE REALLY IS LIKE A HOPELESS LITTLE BROTHER.

RRRING

SAITŌ-SEMPAI

SO I THOUGHT I'D CALL.

JUST WONDERING WHAT YOU WERE DOING.

H-HI.

I WAS ON MY WAY HOME FROM PRACTICE.

WE'RE ALWAYS WALKING HOME AT THE SAME TIME THESE DAYS.

I'M ON MY WAY HOME, TOO.

... DOESN'T INCLUDE ME.

THAT "WE"...

"WE"...

...I WAS THE ONE WHO'S BEEN CLOSEST TO HIM.

EVER SINCE WE WERE LITTLE...

BUT SUD-DENLY...

...THE FAR-THEST AWAY.

I'M...

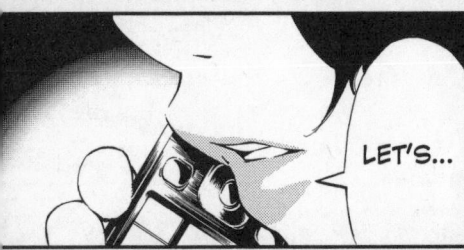

HM?

LET'S...

SEM-PAI.

...GO OUT.

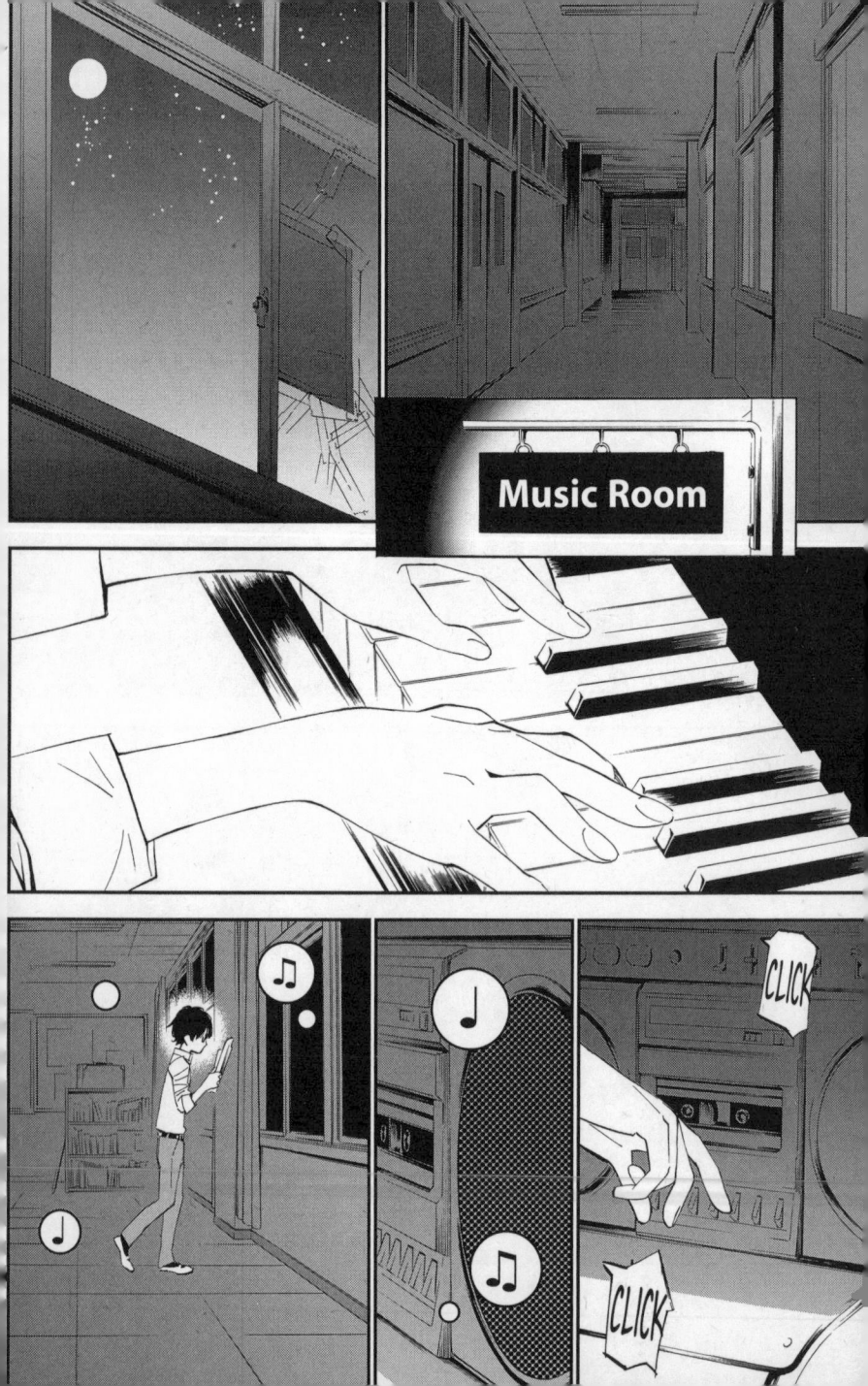

...BY COVERING IT UP WITH DUST AND BOOKS.

SO YOU TRIED TO AVERT YOUR EYES FROM THE ONE THING YOU WANTED TO SEE...

YOU COULDN'T GIVE IT UP.

YOU'RE SAD.

YOU'RE HURTING.

AND I PRETENDED NOT TO NOTICE.

YOU LOVED IT, BUT YOU COULDN'T GET NEAR IT.

YOU YEARNED FOR IT, BUT YOU COULDN'T TOUCH IT.

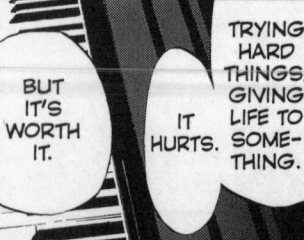

FOR SHAKING THE DUST OFF OF ME.

MY WORLD STARTED TO CHANGE...

...A LONG TIME AGO.

I JUST DIDN'T NOTICE IT.

THANK YOU.

SO...

...THANK YOU.

SINCE THAT DAY...

...FOR COM-ING INTO MY LIFE.

...MY WORLD—EVEN MY KEY-BOARD...

...HAS BEEN FULL OF COLOR.

IN THE DARK OF NIGHT ...

...IT'S AS IF ONLY THE TWO OF US EXIST.

GOOD MORNING, SENSEI.

HERE'S THE LIST OF MUSICIANS COMPETING IN THE MAIHŌ COMPETITION.

LOOK WHERE I MARKED IT.

RUSTLE

I WAITED TWO YEARS FOR THIS.

SHRED

WHAA ?!

HOW'S THAT FOR MOTIVATION?

TREMBLE

TREMBLE

TREMBLE

THE TIME HAS FINALLY COME...

...TO WIPE AWAY MY YEARS OF HUMILIA-TION.

TAKESHI AIZA

I SEE YOU'VE HEARD.

"IT TAKES COURAGE TO SAIL IN UNCHARTED WATERS."
-SNOOPY

I WISH *YOU* WOULD CARRY *ME!*

Chapter 10: The Way Home

MAIDEN IN LOVE WITH BEING IN LOVE.

THIS IS ALL YOUR FAULT, TSU-BAKI!!

WHAT?!

YOU WANNA PIECE OF ME, PUNK?!

IT WOULD BE SO COOL...

...TO HAVE A CUTE BOY CARRY ME HOME.

OH, WHAT AM I SAY-ING?!

NOW WE WOULD LIKE TO BEGIN THE PEP RALLY...

...FOR OUR ATHLETIC CLUBS' DISTRICT TOURNA- MENTS!

TEST- ING.

UH.

THE ATHLETIC TOURNAMENTS ARE STARTING SOON.

FIRST, SOME WORDS OF ENCOURAGEMENT FROM OUR PRINCIPAL.

PASH

HEY!

STARTING WITH THE SOCCER TEAM'S—

AV

FOR TSUBAKI AND WATARI...

YOU'RE A LUCKY LOT TO HAVE BEEN BORN IN THIS GENERATION.

...THE LAST SUMMER OF THEIR MIDDLE SCHOOL CAREERS IS ABOUT TO BEGIN.

NOW, A REPRESENTATIVE FROM EACH TEAM WILL SHOW US THEIR TEAM SPIRIT.

MURMUR

WHAT THE?

?

MUR-MUR

...NEED TO SPEND TIME SEEING THE SKY.

MUSI- CIANS...

WE'RE GOING TO CHEER ON OUR FRIENDS.

NO.

NYAH

WHA —!

NEIN.

THEY'RE PLAYING HERE AT OUR SCHOOL.

ARE WE GOING TO WATCH THE SOCCER TEAM?

THEY HAVE A GOOD PITCHER.

A SOUTH-PAW PITCHING RISE-BALLS.

NICE ONE, TSUBAKI.

THIS IS GOING TO BE A CLOSE GAME.

TSU-BAKIII!

Sumiya. Sumiya. Sumiya.

BUT YOU KNOW...

CON-CEN-TRATE!

SHE'S JUST NOT HER-SELF.

BOO! BOO!

SO EVERY-THING'S PERFECT FOR YOU WITH SPORTS AND LOVE, IS IT?!

THE BALL IS LIKE PUTTY IN YOUR HANDS, EH?

DON'T GET COCKY JUST BECAUSE YOU'RE DATING SAITŌ-SEMPAI!

I SAW YOU WALKING WITH HIM YESTER-DAY!

?!

DON'T GIVE THAT LOOK ...

...TO SOME- BODY ELSE.

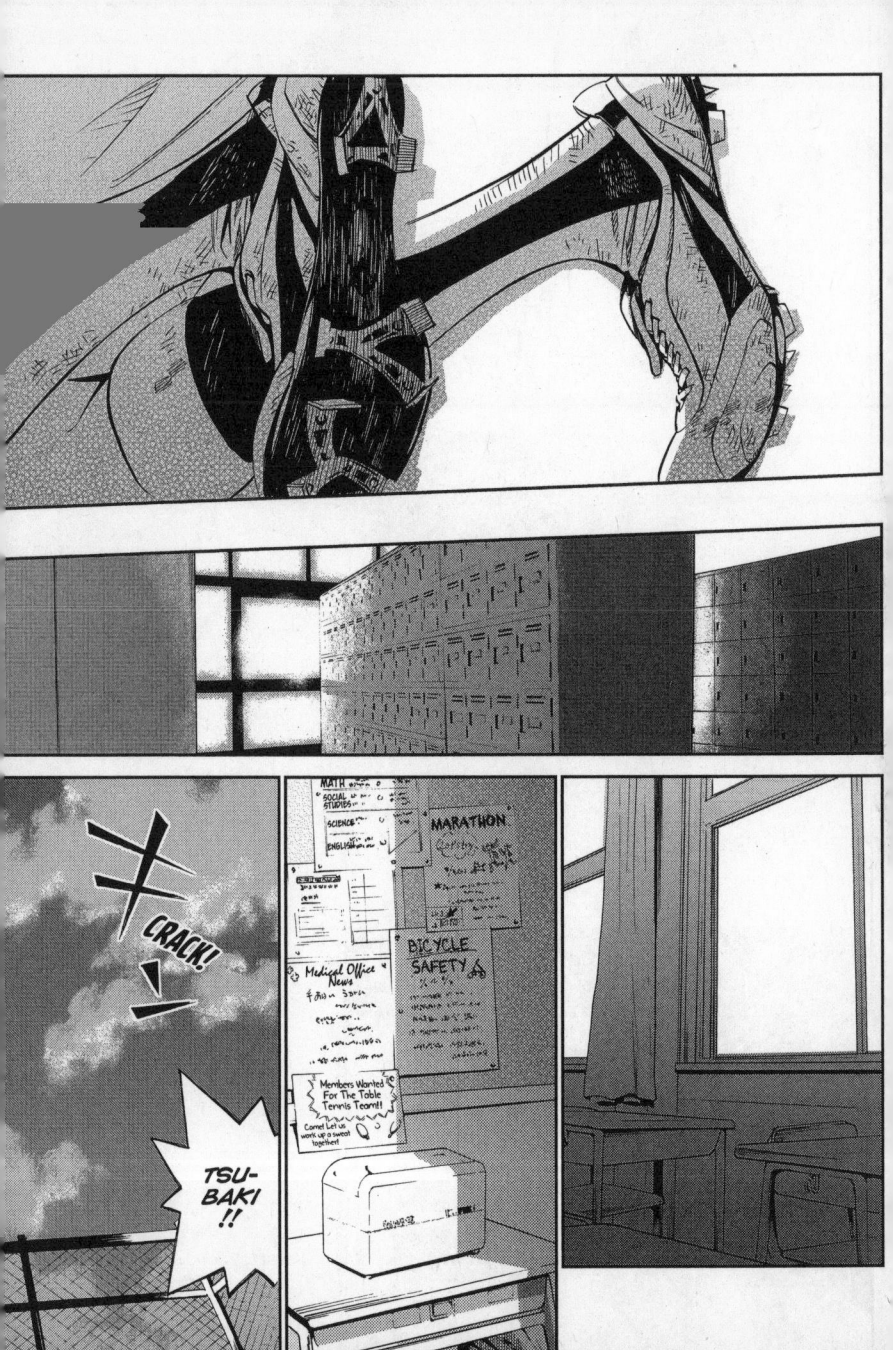

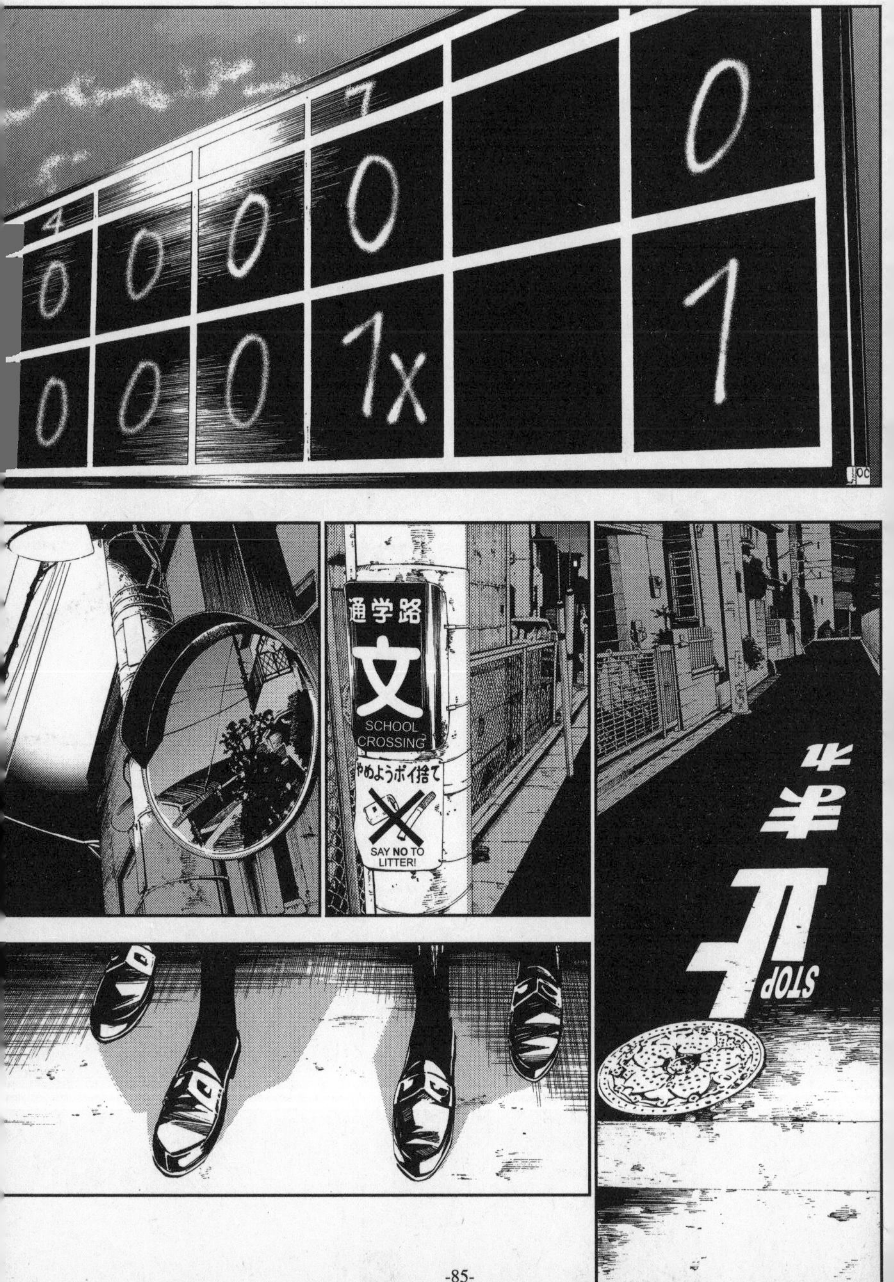

通学路

文

SCHOOL
CROSSING

やめようポイ捨て

SAY NO TO
LITTER!

STOP

GO HAVE YOUR BOYFRIEND CHEER YOU UP.

BUT KASHI-WAGI, YOUR HOUSE IS THIS WAY.

I'M GOING THIS WAY.

TSU-BAKI.

HEY.

...

HEY.

TAP
チョン

NO-BODY'S WATCH-ING.

KŌSEI... THIS IS EMBAR-RASS-ING.

I CAN ALWAYS TELL WHEN YOU'RE SUFFERING IN SILENCE.

HOW LONG DO YOU THINK I'VE KNOWN YOU?

NO ONE *ELSE* FIGURED IT OUT.

...WHERE'S KAO-CHAN?

SHE WENT HOME.

SHE TOLD ME I HAD TO COME SEE YOU ALONE.

YOU HAVEN'T CHANGED AT ALL SINCE WE WERE KIDS.

IT'S JUST LIKE WHEN WE ROLLED DOWN THAT HILL.

...IF YOU DIDN'T TRY TO PUSH THROUGH IT.

IT WOULDN'T SWELL LIKE THAT...

SO...

...YOU DON'T HAVE TO SUFFER IN SILENCE FOR ME.

MY HEART IS A LOT MORE UN-STEADY.

YES, I HAVE.

YOU CAN'T FOOL ME—I KNOW EVERYTHING ABOUT YOU.

DON'T EVEN TRY.

ALL I EVER DO IS MAKE YOU WORRY.

I WANT YOU TO LET ME WORRY ABOUT YOU SOME-TIMES.

I MIGHT BE AN UNRELI-ABLE LITTLE BROTHER...

I'LL DO MY BEST.

SO...

...BUT I'LL DO WHAT I CAN.

YOU REALLY ARE A GIRL, TSUBAKI.

TSU-BAKI.

WHA—!

IN-SULTS!

YOU'RE LIGHTER THAN YOU LOOK.

MAYBE IT'S BECAUSE THE SEASONS ARE CHANGING.

YEAH.

THAT WAS A WEIRD THING TO SAY.

BONK

WH-WHAT'S THAT SUP-POSED TO MEAN?!

WEIR-DO!

THAT HURTS! DON'T HIT ME!

BONK

WHO CARES ABOUT MUSIC?

WHO CARES ABOUT WORDS?

WE HAVE SO MANY...

...SMALL BUT PRECIOUS MEMORIES.

WE HAVE ALL THE LONG YEARS WE SPENT TOGETHER.

NEXT TIME...

HNNH.

NNH.

SCRUNCH

...I'LL CARRY YOU, TSUBAKI.

HELLO ANGEL

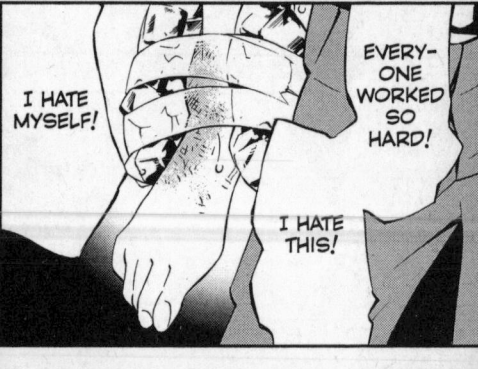

IT'S STRANGE.

SO WHY ARE THE STARS...

...SHINING SO BRIGHTLY?

EVERYTHING SUCKS.

I HATE THAT WE LOST.

I'M SUPER DEPRESSED.

MY FOOT HURTS.

I CAN HARDLY SEE THROUGH ALL THE TEARS.

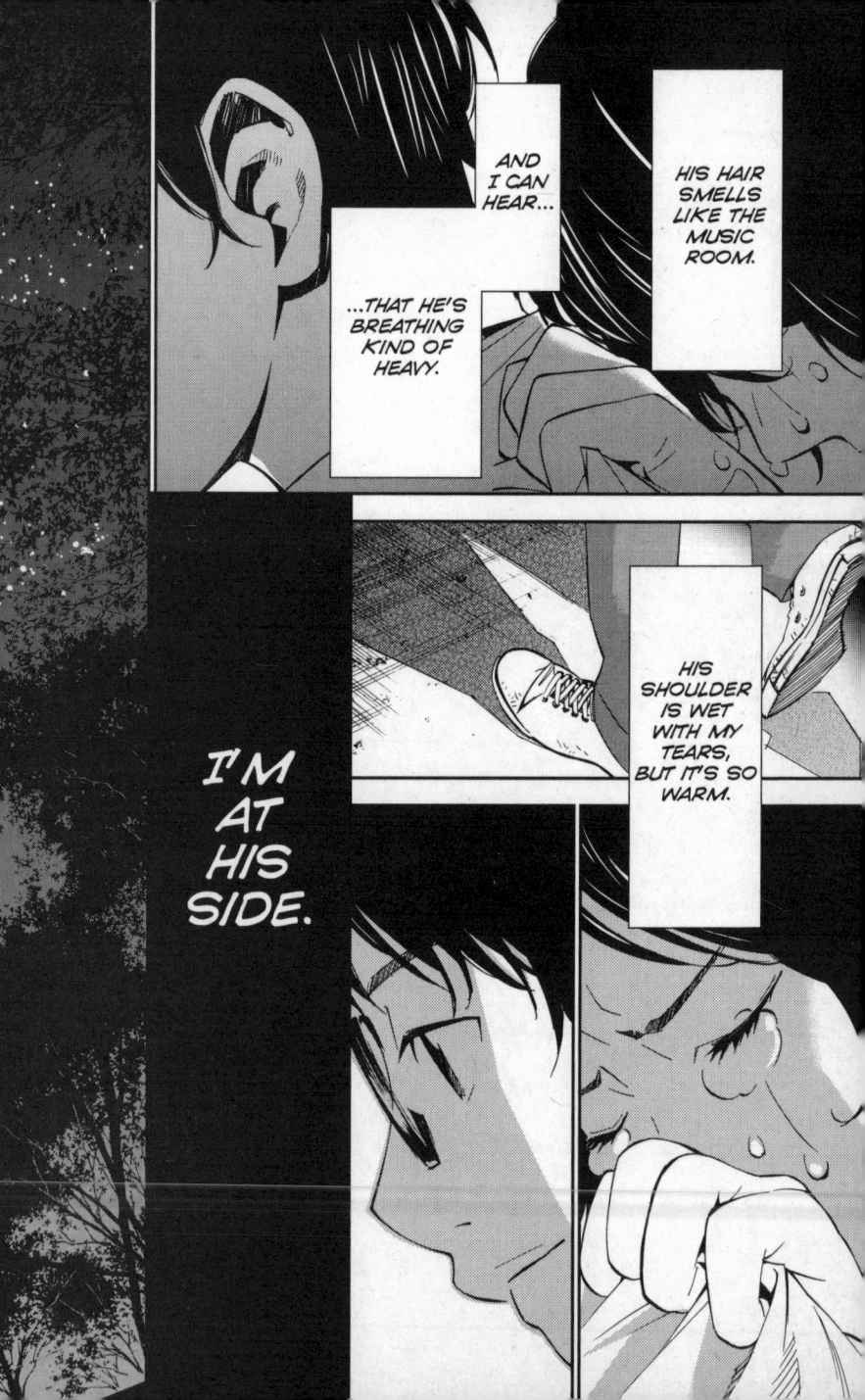

I WISH...

...TIME WOULD STOP RIGHT NOW.

WAAAAH!

WAAAAH!

DON'T PULL MY HAIR.

THE WAY HOME / END

Your Lie in April

I met the girl under full-bloomed cherry blossoms, and my fate has begun to change.

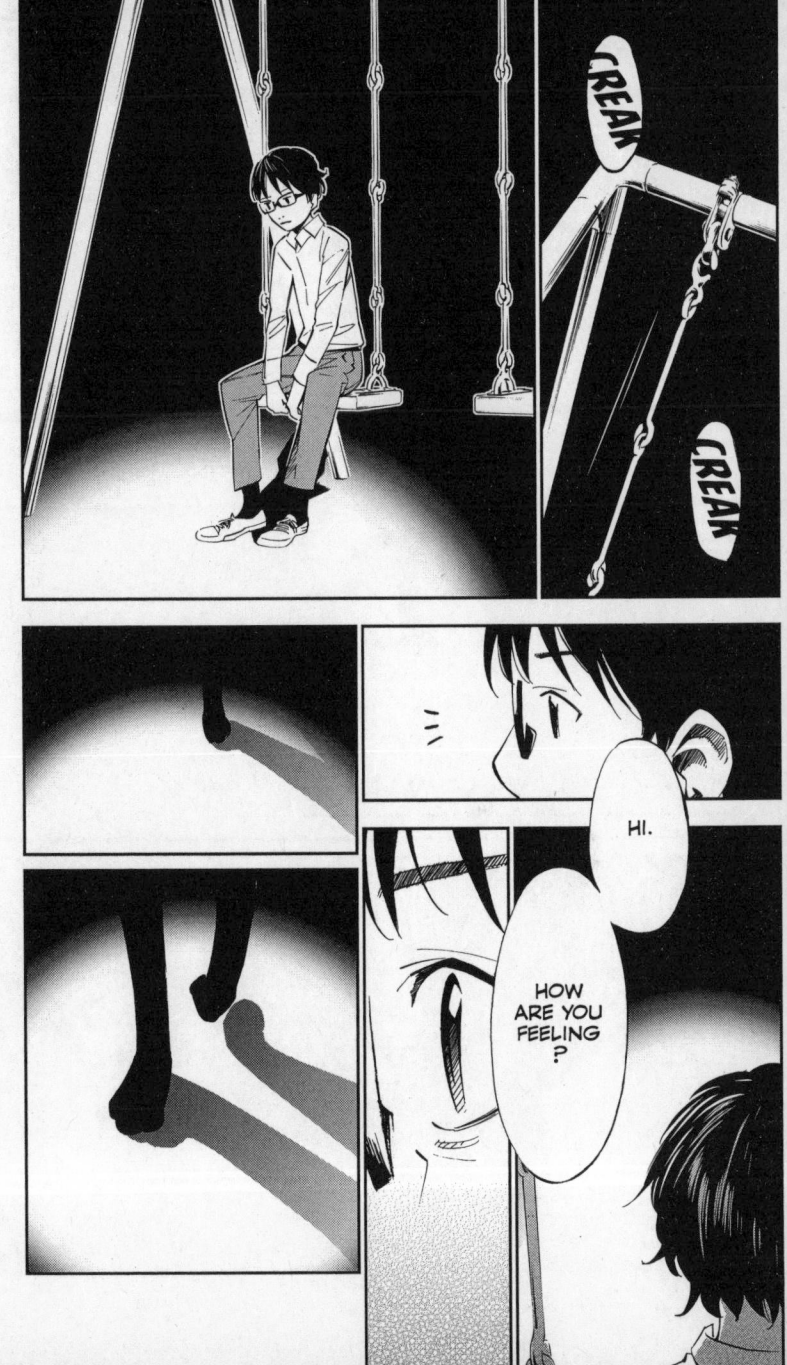

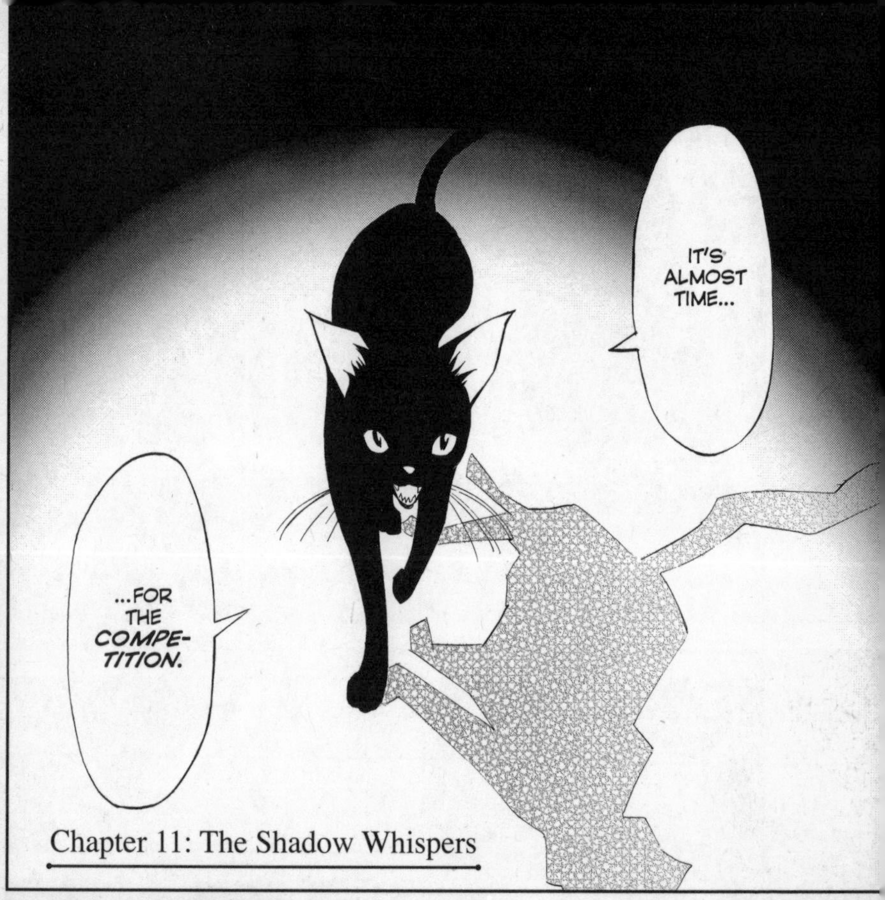

IT'S ALMOST TIME...

...FOR THE *COMPE-TITION.*

Chapter 11: The Shadow Whispers

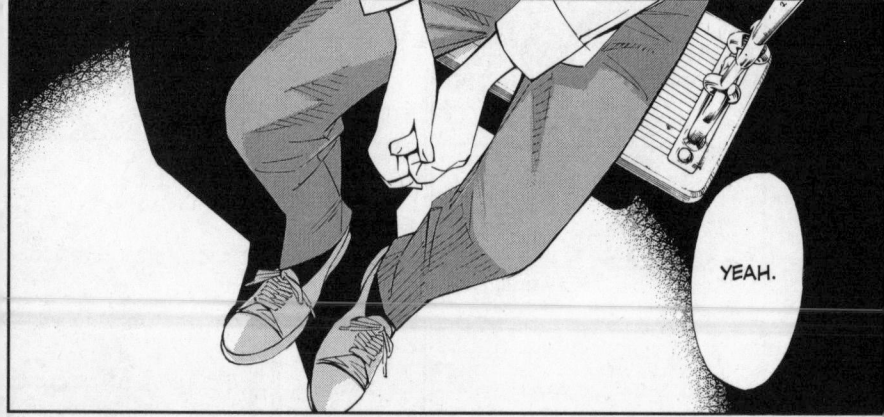

YEAH.

DON'T BE AFRAID.

THERE'S NOTHING TO WORRY ABOUT.

WHO CARES IF YOU EMBAR-RASS YOUR-SELF?

WHO CARES IF EVERY-BODY LAUGHS?

IT'S NOT LIKE THEY'RE GOING TO *GET RID* OF YOU.

PURR

MEOW!

YOU'RE NO BEETHOVEN, AFTER ALL.

PURR

PURR

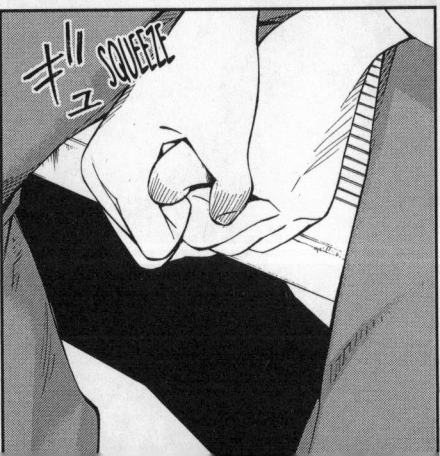

SQUEEZE

WHERE ARE YOU?

NOW.

CREAK

B-DMP

ARE YOU READY TO START YOUR JOURNEY?

HE LOOKS DREAMY WHEN HE'S CRUSHED, TOO

YOU WERE SO CLOSE.

THAT'S TOO BAD.

SO WATARI LOST, TOO.

WATARIII!

DON'T CRY.

WE DID OUR BEST.

HNNH.

YOU WERE AWESOME.

THANKS FOR CHEERING ME ON.

COME ON, WE HAVE TO CONGRATULATE THE OTHER TEAM.

I MISSED MY CHANCE TO BE A STAR.

LET'S GO HOME.

HE REALLY WAS AWESOME.

WE'LL TRY AGAIN IN HIGH SCHOOL.

WA-TARI.

IT'S ALL UP TO YOU NOW.

?

WHERE'S WA-TARI?

SAID HE'S GONNA TAKE A DUMP.

THANKS FOR THE GOOD GAME!

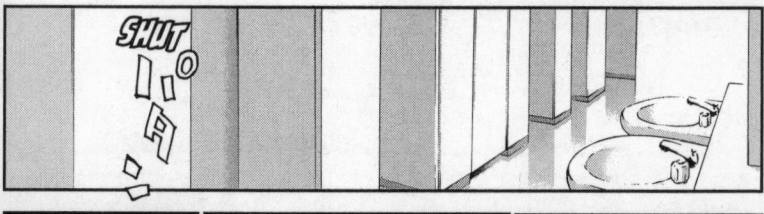

SHUT

DAM-MIT.

SO I WON'T BE A STAR UNTIL HIGH SCHOOL.

SOB...

SOB...

DAM-MIT.

DAM-MIT.

FOR WATARI AND TSU-BAKI...

...THE LAST TOUR-NAMENTS OF MIDDLE SCHOOL WERE OVER.

I SWEAR I WON'T LOSE NEXT TIME.

Library

T-TAP

TAP

TAP

RAR

ARI-MA!

STOP THAT NOISE! CLASS IS IN SESSION !!

!!

T-TMP

TMP

TMP

T-TAP

TAP

HUFF

HUFF

...BOTH SHINED SO BRIGHT-LY.

...AND TSU-BAKI...

WA-TARI...

THREE LAPS TO GO!

YOU WERE THERE...

...WITH THAT COM-MANDING PRES-ENCE.

AND YOU, TOO.

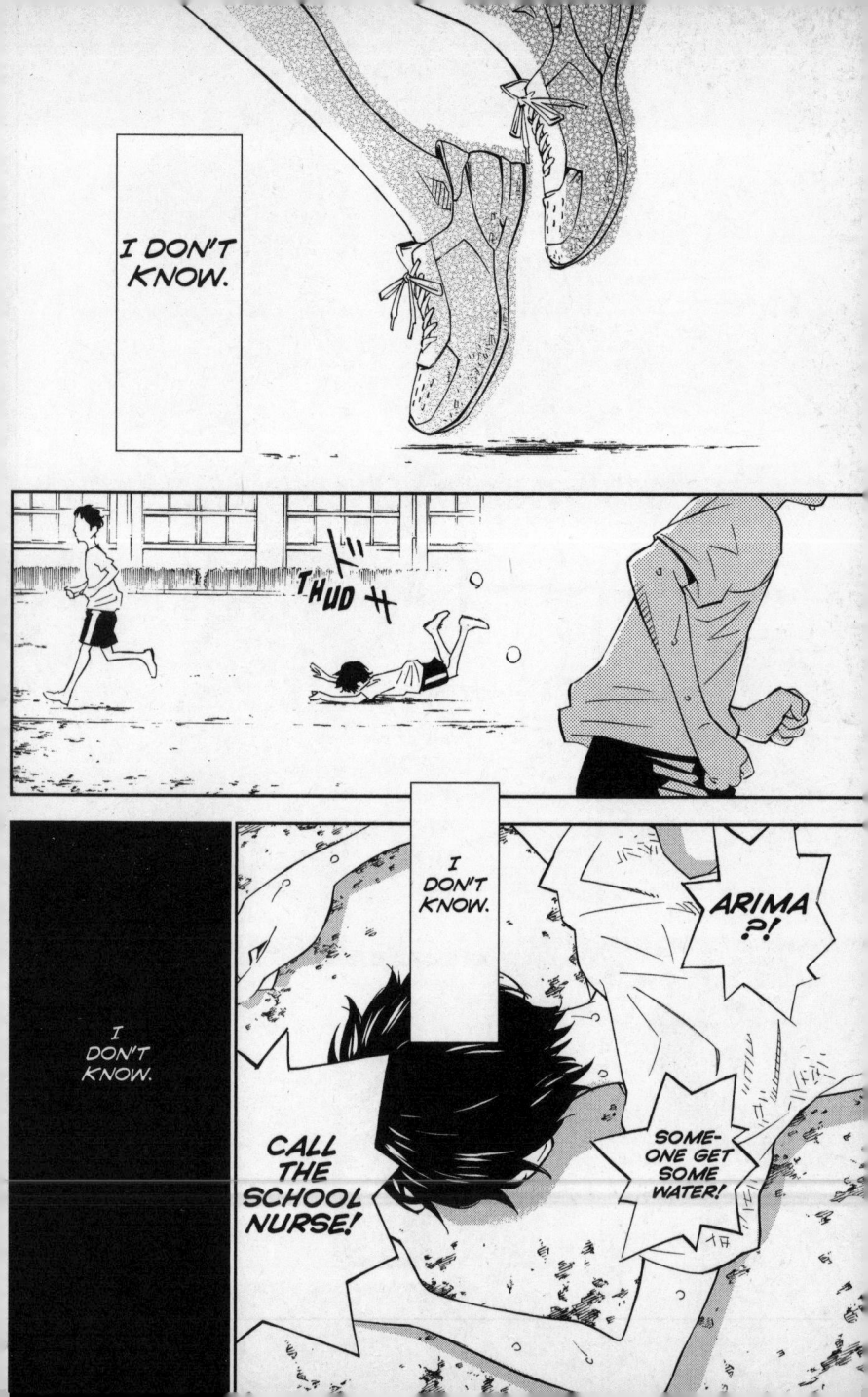

UNBE-
LIEV-
ABLE!!

YOU
PASSED
OUT
BECAUSE
YOU
HADN'T
EATEN
ANY-
THING?!

IT WAS
A FIVE-
PACK.

BUT
I WAS
FINE ONCE
I ATE
THE EGG
SAND-
WICHES
TSUBAKI
GAVE ME.

FIVE
?!

SLURRRP
ちゅ

I
COULDN'T
HELP IT. I
WAS SO
ABSORBED
IN MY
PRACTIC-
ING.

YOUR
BODY IS
YOUR
GREATEST
ASSET!

WHERE ARE YOU?

COUGH!

MILK

ARE YOU OKAY?!

OVER THERE!

THERE'S A PUBLIC RESTROOM!!

BLEGH!

COUGH!

WHEN I WAS A KID...

...I HAD A BLACK CAT.

OJI PARK

SINCE THAT DAY...

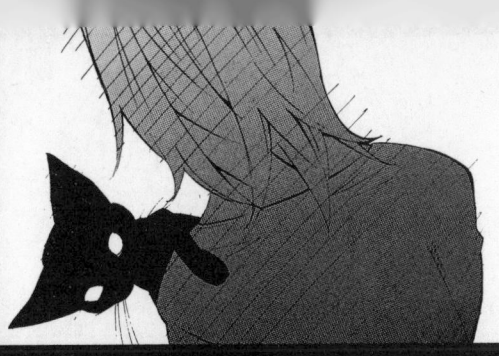

...I'VE ALWAYS BEEN IN MOM'S SHADOW.

YOU LIKE EGG SANDWICHES.

YOU'RE A LITTLE JEALOUS OF WATARI-KUN'S POPULARITY.

YOU CAN'T SAY NO TO TSUBAKI-CHAN.

YOU LIKE MILK WITH THE CUTE COW LOGO.

YOU...

...ARE NOT YOUR MOTHER'S SHADOW.

YOU'RE A TERRIBLE ATHLETE.

YOU HAVE MORE OF A SWEET TOOTH THAN I WOULD HAVE THOUGHT.

THE GREAT TEACHERS ARE ALWAYS SAYING.

GET A DEEP UNDERSTANDING OF THEM.

"THE HISTORICAL BACKGROUND."

"THE STYLE OF THE TIMES."

"STUDY THE COMPOSER'S INTENTIONS."

WE DON'T WEAR THOSE FUNNY HAIRSTYLES.

I MEAN, WE WEREN'T BORN IN THE BAROQUE ERA.

BUT DON'T YOU THINK THERE'S ONLY SO FAR YOU CAN GO WITH THAT?

AND THAT'S IMPORTANT.

SOME-TIMES...

...YOU SAY SOME REALLY SMART THINGS.

OW!

OW!

WHACK

WHACK

WHACK

WHAT DO YOU MEAN "SOME-TIMES" ?!

I'M TRYING TO EN-COURAGE YOU HERE!

FROM THE HEART...

CHARLIE BROWN.

WHO SAID THAT?

THE HANDS OF A PIANIST.

BIG, BONY HANDS.

BLUSH

YOUR HAND IS HAPPY TO BE TOUCHING ME.

BWA?!

SEE? I KNEW IT.

?

IT'S JUST ITCHING TO PLAY THE PIANO.

...ALL THE UN-CER-TAINTY...

AFTER ALL THE WOR-RYING...

...YOU FINALLY GET TO AN ANSWER. AND IT'S FUNNY...

...ALL THE SUF-FER-ING...

...HOW SIMPLE IT IS.

HOW'S IT GOING?

HI.

NO.

YOU STILL CAN'T HEAR THE MUSIC, CAN YOU?

IT'S ALL RIGHT.

IT'S TOMOR-ROW, ISN'T IT?

YOUR COMPETI-TION.

NO, IT'S NOT.

THAT'S... NOT AN ANSWER.

IT LOOKS LIKE YOU'RE READY.

...

YEAH.

I'M SURE SHE'LL BE THERE, TOO.

TOMORROW IS GOING TO BE A LONG DAY.

SO TODAY...

...GET PLENTY OF REST.

WHOA.

THIS PLACE IS *HUGE*.

IS THIS WHERE THEY'RE HAVING IT?

OH!!

FIDGET

FIDGET

WILL HE BE OKAY?

WOBBLE

WOBBLE

WOBBLE

WELL, I'M OFF.

ZOOM

WHAT?!

WHAT?!

OH, WOW!! I HAVE TO TELL HIM!

KŌSEI!

YOU'RE GOING THE WRONG WAY!

...AND MY COMPE-TITION BEGINS.

A CHANCE ENCOUN-TER WITH MY PAST...

THE SHADOW WHISPERS / END

"WHEN YOU'RE DEPRESSED, IT ALWAYS HELPS TO LEAN YOUR HEAD ON YOUR ARM. ARMS LIKE TO FEEL USEFUL."
                    -CHARLIE BROWN

Music Competitio[n]
Award Winners

THERE IT IS! THAT'S MY NAME!

YES!

CLAMOR

CLAMOR

CLAMOR

Inoha
Music Competition
Award Winners

I HATE TO ADMIT IT, BUT THEY WERE WONDERFUL.

MY LITTLE ONE DIDN'T WIN AGAIN.

CLAMOR

I'M GONNA TAKE A PICTURE.

CLAMOR

BUT I FELT LIKE I DID SO WELL.

AWW, I'M NOT ON THERE.

Igawa, Emi
[A]iza, Takeshi
[...]o, Kaz[...]a

EMI IGAWA-CHAN.

AND TAKESHI AIZA-KUN.

CHATTER

I KNEW IT WASN'T A GOOD IDEA TO PUT THEM TOGETHER.

WE'LL BE IN SIXTH GRADE NEXT YEAR, SO LET'S DO OUR BEST!

CHATTER

...WENT STRAIGHT HOME...

...WITHOUT EVEN LOOKING AT THE RESULTS, LIKE THEY DIDN'T EVEN MATTER.

RRRAAARRR

PEW!

HA!

MAKE UP YOUR MIND.

THOUGH THAT'D MAKE ME MAD, TOO!

YOU COULD AT LEAST BE A LITTLE HAPPY, PUNK!!

PROBABLY...

...NOT EVEN IN HIMSELF.

HE'S JUST NOT INTERESTED.

NOT IN US, NOT IN ANYONE.

KŌSEI ARIMA'S NAME...

LIVING FOR COMPETITION.

THE HUMAN METRONOME.

LIKE A DIGITAL CLOCK...

...NOT EVEN OFF BY A SPLIT-SECOND.

HIS MOTHER'S MARIONETTE.

...LIVES IN INFAMY.

SLAVE TO THE SCORE.

NO LINGERING NOTES.

WHO SAID THAT?! I'LL KNOCK 'EM INTO NEXT WEEK!!

SHH!

SHH!

WAS IT YOU?!

WHAT?! WELL, BRING IT ON!!

WHAM RRR-RRA-AAA-HH!

YOU'RE ONE OF THE FIRST PERFORM-ERS.

GO GET CHANGED.

KEEP YOUR WITS ABOUT YOU.

HE FOR-GOT ALL ABOUT US!!

RRR-RAAAA-RRR!

DAMN THAT ARIMA!

GRRR!

CALM DOWN, TAKESHI.

WHOA, DOWN, BOY.

HE NEVER KNEW US.

...ARIMA DIDN'T FORGET US.

BE-SIDES ...

HE HASN'T CHANGED A BIT...

I DON'T LIKE IT.

HE HAS SUCH GOOD TECHNIQUE.

...HE GETS ALL KINDS OF SPECIAL TREATMENT.

JUST BECAUSE HIS MOTHER LEARNED FROM A GREAT PIANO MASTER...

BUT HE'S PLAYING SUCH BORING PIECES.

...IN THE LAST TWO YEARS.

VVVVN

RRRAAARRR

RUMBLE

RUMBLE

RUMBLE

RUMBLE

AND A PERSON CAN'T CHANGE MUCH IN TWO YEARS.

I FIRST MET HIM WHEN WE WERE IN THIRD GRADE.

I REACHED OUT AS FAR AS MY HAND WOULD GO.

AND JUST WHEN I THOUGHT I HAD HIM...

I KEPT TELLING MYSELF, "NEXT TIME." "NEXT TIME."

LIKE A MIRAGE.

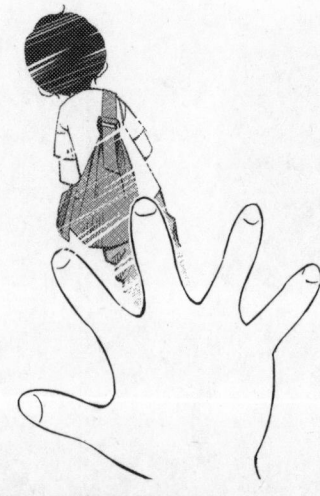

...HE WAS FAR AWAY AGAIN.

TODAY, HE'S FINALLY BACK...

...WHERE HE BE-LONGS.

LIKE A MAGI-CIAN'S DOVE...

...HE'D VANISH.

NUMBER 3.

YŪKO KAWANAKA-SAN. GET READY TO GO ON.

MUTTER

MUTTER

MUTTER

FS-HH

FS-HH

BLEGH!

TOILET

BLEEE-ARGH!

THEY'RE...

...ALL SCARED.

CLACK

LAST YEAR'S CHAMPION.

TAKESHI AIZA.

CREAK

CLAP

CLAP

CLAP

CLAP

AND CHOPIN'S ÉTUDES...

THERE HE IS.

NOW WE CAN FINALLY HEAR SOME REAL PLAYING.

...ARE BACH'S WELL-TEMPERED CLAVIER, BOOK 1: PRELUDE AND FUGUE NO. 13,

THE TWO PIECES HE SELECTED...

Takeshi Hasa-M... J.S.Ba...

...OPUS 10, NO. 4.

SNAP

Chopi... Op.1

THIS...

AN UN-SHAK-ABLE TRUNK...

...TOW-ERING ABOVE ITS ROOTS.

...IS TAKESHI AIZA'S CHOPIN.

SHE'S LISTENING TO SOMEONE ELSE PLAY?

I'VE NEVER SEEN A KID DO THAT.

BRAVE GIRL.

STAFF

WHOA.

CRUNCH

TAKE-SHI.

ARI-MA.

B-DMP

B-DMP

B-DMP

HE'S LISTENING TO SOMEONE ELSE?

NO 1

ENOUGH

NOW...

...IT'S YOUR TURN.

YOUR LIE IN APRIL, TO BE CONTINUED

YOUR LIE IN APRIL FEATURED MUSIC

JOHANN SEBASTIAN BACH'S THE WELL-TEMPERED CLAVIER & CHOPIN'S ÉTUDES

The Well-Tempered Clavier is a collection of pieces by Bach, the father of all music, for the instruction of his sons and students. There are two volumes of 24 pieces each, covering all major and minor keys. Each piece is composed of two smaller ones: a prelude and a fugue.

Chopin's Études were written after the pattern of Bach's Clavier, as a collection of 24 practice pieces. The collection contains many works, such as "Tristesse," "Black Keys," and "Revolutionary," that overflow with beautiful melodies and harmonies which could only have been composed by the poet of the piano.

Both collections are unavoidable stops on the path of a young person aspiring to be a pianist, and they are required playing for a wide range of competitions, from school to international level.

JOHANN SEBASTIAN BACH'S WELL-TEMPERED CLAVIER, BOOK 1: PRELUDE AND FUGUE NO. 13 IN F-SHARP MAJOR BWV858

This prelude, consisting of two simple melodies, was composed in the slightly unusual time signature of 12/16. This combines the steady rhythm of four-beat time with the lilt of three-beat time, and this, coupled with the major key sound, creates a warm, comfortable atmosphere.

The following fugue progresses with three intertwining melodies. What makes this fugue a challenge is that, in order to play three melodies with two hands, the pianist must play multiple melodies with a single hand. Another important point in performing this piece is that the pianist must reconstruct the dizzying development of the piece by playing the sonorous, expressive sections and the sad, mournful sections all with the same limited set of musical patterns.

(Pianist Masanori Sugano, lecturer at Tokyo University of the Arts and Musashino Academia Musicae)

Continued On The Next Page.

YOUR LIE IN APRIL FEATURED MUSIC

CHOPIN'S ÉTUDES OP. 10, NO. 4 IN C-SHARP MINOR

Among Chopin's works, which are known for their sweetness, this piece is like a very angry and excitable man who has suddenly been shoved onto center stage. It is a highly technical piece, including high-speed passages that alternate from the right hand to the left, several leaps to distant chords, and a wide contrast between piano (soft) and forte (loud).

It's easy to overlook, hiding in the shadows of the difficult technical elements of this piece, but the important thing musically is how the pianist plays the prominent chords. Of course the right and left hands need to be balanced, but there must also be balance between the finer notes and the relaxed chord progression, and whether or not a pianist can draw out that balance is an important key to the success of the performance.

(Pianist Masanori Sugano, lecturer at Tokyo University of the Arts and Musashino Academia Musicae)

Watch it on YouTube (Search "Monthly Shonen Magazine Your Lie in April Featured Music")

Special Thanks:

AKINORI ŌSAWA

MASANORI SUGANO

RIEKO IKEDA

KAORI YAMAZAKI

Translation Notes

Zombie, page 24

Specifically, the girl who is startled by Kōsei's shambling down the hall thinks she's seen a *kyonshi*, or *jiangshi*, as it is known in Chinese. A *jiangshi*, meaning literally "collapsed corpse," is an undead creature from Chinese folklore, often described as a "hopping" zombie or vampire.

The go-home club, page 65

In Japan, almost every student in school is in a club (at some schools, it's required). Usually, the clubs are divided into two categories: *undōbu*, or athletic clubs (including all the sports teams), and *bunkabu*, or culture clubs (including art, music, literature, etc.). There is one final category of clubs, and that's the category for people who haven't joined any club—the *kitakubu*, or go-home club. Members of this club use their extracurricular time to go home.

ATTACK ON TITAN

Winner of a 2011 Kodansha Manga Award

Humanity has been decimated!

A century ago, the bizarre creatures known as Titans devoured most of the world's population, driving the remainder into a walled stronghold. Now, the appearance of an immense new Titan threatens the few humans left, and one restless boy decides to seize the chance to fight for his freedom, and the survival of his species!

KC KODANSHA COMICS

Praise for the anime:

"The show provides a pleasant window on the highs and lows of young love with two young people who are first timers at the real thing."

–The Fandom Post

"Always it is smarter, more poetic, more touching, just plain better than you think it is going to be."

–Anime News Network

SAY I LOVE YOU.

KC KODANSHA COMICS

Mei Tachibana has no friends — and says she doesn't need them!

But everything changes when she accidentally roundhouse kicks the most popular boy in school! However, Yamato Kurosawa isn't angry in the slightest— in fact, he thinks his ordinary life could use an unusual girl like Mei. But winning Mei's trust will be a tough task. How long will she refuse to say, "I love you"?

NO.6

A PERFECT LIFE IN A PERFECT CITY

For Shion, an elite student in the technologically sophisticated city No. 6, life is carefully choreographed. One fateful day, he takes a misstep, sheltering a fugitive his age from a typhoon. Helping this boy throws Shion's life down a path to discovering the appalling secrets behind the "perfection" of No. 6.

KC
KODANSHA
COMICS

PRAISE FOR THE ANIME!

"This series never fails to put a smile on my face."
—Dramatic Reviews

"A very funny look at what happens when two strange and strangely well-suited people try to navigate the thorny path to true love together."
—Anime News Network

My Little Monster

OPPOSITES ATTRACT...MAYBE?
Haru Yoshida is feared as an unstable and violent "monster." Mizutani Shizuku is a grade-obsessed student with no friends. Fate brings these two together to form the most unlikely pair. Haru firmly believes he's in love with Mizutani and she firmly believes he's insane.

KC
KODANSHA
COMICS

A Kodansha Comics Trade Paperback Original
Your Lie in April volume 3 copyright © 2012 Naoshi Arakawa
English translation copyright © 2015 Naoshi Arakawa

Published in the United States by Kodansha Comics, an imprint of Kodansha USA Publishing, LLC, New York.

Publication rights for this English edition arranged through Kodansha Ltd, Tokyo.

ISBN 978-1-63236-173-8

Special thanks:
Akinori Osawa, Rieko Ikeda, and Kaori Yamazaki

Printed in the United States of America.

www.kodanshacomics.com

9 8 7 6 5 4 3 2 1
Translation: Alethea and Athena Nibley
Lettering: Scott Brown
Editing: Ben Applegate
Kodansha Comics edition cover design by Phil Balsman

TOMARE! STOP

You're going the wrong way!

Manga is a completely different type of reading experience.

To start at the beginning, Go to the end!

That's right! Authentic manga is read the traditional Japanese way—from right to left, exactly the opposite of how American books are read. It's easy to follow: Just go to the other end of the book and read each page—and each panel—from right side to left side, starting at the top right. Now you're experiencing manga as it was meant to be!